SAVING YOUR RELAT

WHO'S TALKING NOW?

The Owl Or The Crocodile

SEYMOUR BOORSTEIN, M.D.

Illustrated by Elizabeth Boorstein

AuthorHouse™
1663 Liberty Drive
Bloomington, IN 47403
www.authorhouse.com
Phone: 1-800-839-8640

First published by AuthorHouse   09/22/2011

ISBN: 978-1-4567-2829-8 (sc)

Printed in the United States of America

Any people depicted in stock imagery provided by Thinkstock are models,
and such images are being used for illustrative purposes only.
Certain stock imagery © Thinkstock.

This book is printed on acid-free paper.

Because of the dynamic nature of the Internet, any Web addresses or links contained in this book may have changed
since publication and may no longer be valid. The views expressed in this work are solely those of the author and do not
necessarily reflect the views of the publisher, and the publisher hereby disclaims any responsibility for them.

authorHOUSE®

DEDICATION PAGE

To my mother Dena, who taught me how to work hard

To my father Harry, who taught me about gentle sweetness

To my wife Sylvia, who taught me about love and loving

I would like to dedicate this book to the healing of the world,

starting with your relationship.

ACKNOWLEDGEMENTS

I cannot find enough words to fully express my gratitude to my friend Dawna Markova for her encouragement, guidance and support as I wrote this book. It was Dawna who helped me make the decision to put my work together in this form. She thought it would be valuable for many couples and, knowing that I am not naturally a writer, promised that she would coach me if I agreed. She was incredibly available to me throughout the writing process, helped me shape and organize my ideas, supported me when my courage waned, and celebrated with me as things came together. I could not have written this without her.

I also am grateful for my friends Lewis Richmond, Jenny Wade, Suzie Hobbins, and Ken Ring for their support and for their receptive, appreciative listening as I explained this project to them over the many years of its development.

And of course, collaborating with my daughter Elizabeth, who provided all of the wonderful drawings, was a complete joy. Her offer to design cartoons was the spark that set the whole project in motion.

My son Michael did a masterful job supporting me in the creation of this book, including formatting, collating and editing. Linda Buchanan and Beth Haden reviewed and edited the manuscript and helped to shape the current form. A special thanks to my granddaughter Grace, who helped with editorial revisions.

A Simple Model for Healing Relationships

My name is Seymour Boorstein and I have been a practicing psychiatrist for more than 50 years. I am also a teacher and supervisor at the University of California, San Francisco, School of Medicine. In retrospect, had I been aware of the concepts that I present in this book earlier in my practice, I would have been far more effective in helping my patients.

In 1992 I heard Dr. Dan Goleman give a lecture on the research he was doing that ultimately led to his very important book, <u>Emotional Intelligence.</u> He described what I call our two brains: the primitive limbic system, and our more evolved cortical and neocortical system. He said that the limbic system impulses travel many times faster than the neocortical impulses. The result is that the limbic system highjacks the thought process because it initiates action based on its agenda before the neocortical system has a chance to respond wisely.

I realized that many couples find themselves in destructive exchanges without really knowing how they got there because it all happens so quickly. I recognized that couples become confused when the limbic system's speed and lack of insight takes priority over the slower reasoning of the more mature cortical system.

To make these concepts easier and more useable for couples, I decided to characterize each of the two systems as an animal. I called the limbic system, historically referred to as the reptilian brain, a *crocodile*. For the wiser, slower thinking neo-cortical system, I used an *owl*.

Since then I have seen that this seemingly simple model can be extremely helpful in examining and then solving the problems that couples have. I believe it can also be useful for relationships between parents and children, employers and employees, as well as between friends.

For many years in my work with couples, I have developed techniques to prevent the crocodile brain from destructively overpowering the owl brain so that couples can move toward healing their relationships. This book contains

the tools, methods, and strategies that I have found to be most effective. In order to demonstrate exactly how using these techniques can work for you, I will show you through examples some typical struggles that couples have.

The stories are compilations and distillations of the conversations I have had with couples over many sessions. Many times I combine important points from other couples into one to make certain points more illustrative of what I am teaching. The dialogue has

been stylized to make the stories fit within the space confines of this book. So, although you are not reading exact dialogues, the exchanges are faithful to the tools offered.

It would be optimal for both parties in a relationship to read and use the techniques I describe. However, even if only one of the parties makes positive changes, it will have a positive effect on both people in the relationship. I sometimes explain to my patients that relationships are like see-saws. What one person in the relationship does always affects the other.

The model I present in these pages is easy for anyone to understand. If you're in a challenging relationship of any kind, I think it will help you to avoid your destructive crocodile ways and encourage your wise owl's caring and helpful direction. As long as your relationship does not involve violence or addictions, which require more specific professional therapeutic interventions, this book will provide you with skills that you and your partner can use to make your life together more gratifying.

Chapter 1

THE OWL AND THE CROCODILE

Let's now examine the main characters, the owl and the crocodile, in greater depth.

The owl represents your best, highest, and most mature values - the part of you that is loving, kind, and compassionate. The owl nurtures your self-esteem, cares about the feelings and needs of others, and thinks things through slowly and carefully. The owl lives in the brain's neo-cortex.

The owl's agenda constantly changes as different skills, capacities, wisdoms and humor develop. As these skills become refined, the owl can help a person develop a satisfying career or work that is gratifying, and contribute to the wellbeing of others.

As adolescents and young adults move towards intimacy and companionship with a partner, their owls develop the ability to recognize and accept or appreciate a partner's different points of view. Intimate adult relationships include the desire to nurture one's partner emotionally and physically beyond the most basic survival needs of food and shelter. This can extend beyond one's partner or family, to include all living beings. What I call "The Wise Old Owl" is the part of the brain of a mature adult with a sense of meaning and purpose in life, moral principles, and the courage to live up to them.

The crocodile represents the self-centered part of your nature. It is powerful and reacts quickly. This can be useful if you are driving and need a fast reaction to avoid a collision; but in a relationship, this quick reaction is destructive. The crocodile lives in the brain's limbic system.

The crocodile's main job is to make sure you don't die. Depending on circumstances, the crocodile will either fight, flee, or freeze. Being cunning, it will often try to rationalize its selfish actions and words as being right, justified, and even appropriate. To make sure that it survives, the crocodile will express sexual feelings without caring much about the feelings of its partner. The crocodile has a strong sense of entitlement and is without morals. Here are some of the slogans that the crocodile operates with: "Shoot first and ask questions later," "All is fair in lust and war" and "What's mine is mine and what's yours is mine."

The crocodile lives in the limbic, sub-cortical structure of the brain. We need this survival system in our daily lives. As I have mentioned, it is designed to be protective. Its style is determined by our genes and our early upbringing.

The size and strength of your crocodile is influenced by what you inherited from either one or both of your parents. If your mom and dad had a "short fuse" or showed a great deal of rage, then there is a strong possibility that you may also have those tendencies. In addition, if you experienced physical or psychological trauma as a child, it is likely you will have an overactive crocodile upsetting the balance of your mind when you become an adult. Regardless of the relative strengths of your owl and crocodile, practicing the techniques described in this book will strengthen the owl so it can be the one talking first.

Even though the owl neo-cortical system receives 95% of the information arriving from the senses and the crocodile limbic system only gets 5%, if the crocodile interprets the information as frightening, it winds up making 100% of the verbal and/or action decisions because it reacted first. This faster reaction speed of the crocodile is a problem because the crocodile begins to talk before the owl. Since the crocodile is not kind or caring, its quick response leads to conversations and actions that are full of negative words and emotions.

Dr. John Gottman, a noted relationship researcher, has pointed out that when negative behavior dominates a relationship, the relationship will probably fail. Unfortunately, the present divorce rate is very high, as is the suffering it brings to those affected by the breakup, especially the children. Anyone reading this book can expect to learn how to transform negative feelings (ranging from minor irritations to rage) into ways that are more friendly, caring, and loving.

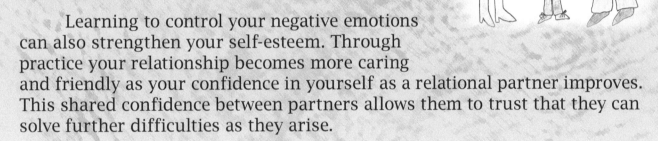

Learning to control your negative emotions can also strengthen your self-esteem. Through practice your relationship becomes more caring and friendly as your confidence in yourself as a relational partner improves. This shared confidence between partners allows them to trust that they can solve further difficulties as they arise.

In general, when I see couples or individuals in my office on their first visit, their crocodiles are dominant. In most relationships, it is best to have the owl be in charge of the interaction and do the "talking;" otherwise the crocodile may misinterpret the situation as life-threatening, and will send an emergency signal for you, via the release of the hormone adrenalin into your body, to get ready to fight or flee.

In life we see the owl and the crocodile at work all around us: high profile people such as politicians, sports celebrities, and actors, who sometimes surprise us and discredit themselves when they are shown to be involved in illegal business affairs or illicit sexual adventures. It is sad to see how crocodile urges, greed or sex, unrecognized, can overwhelm thoughtful owls.

In thoughtful, mature adults the drive to succeed in one's work and the desire for sexual intimacy is normal. Under the supervision of the owl, the drive to succeed is modulated by ethics, and the drive for intimacy is supervised by the owl's capacity for compassion and empathy.

The Supersensitive Neural Network: How the Crocodile Can Take Over

The **Supersensitive Neural Network**, which I will abbreviate from now on as SNN, is a term that I created which refers to the neural circuits that, because of past traumas experienced, become more "on guard" than usual. The reaction by the limbic system (crocodile) becomes stronger and faster each time it is activated. For example, a soldier who has been attacked many times quickly develops a reaction to even the slightest sight or sound with very fast fight or flight reactions. However, when this same soldier, no longer in danger, hears the sound of a car back-firing, his **SNN** may react by preparing to fight or flee. This reaction is a trait of what we commonly call Post Traumatic Stress Disorder (PTSD).

These **SNN** patterns get stronger with repeated negative experiences. The crocodile, with its boosted **SNN**, evaluates every situation that arises in relationships to see if it needs to protect itself. When the crocodile is frightened, the speed of its reaction takes over and, if unchecked, it begins talking or acting unwisely.

Noted neuroscientist Dr. Joseph LeDoux feels that the memories of early interactions are stored in our brains as rough and wordless blueprints. This can explain the puzzling experience of an angry outburst that has no logical basis. A person's fight or flight reaction can come from a time in life when they couldn't really understand what was happening, yet had a strong emotional response. Dr. LeDoux calls these "precognitive emotions." In this way, our crocodile's **SNN** colors what we think and do.

For me, growing up with a very critical mother, my crocodile was always "on guard", and thus is very strong. Now when I lecture to large audiences, I look out over the audience and my crocodile tells me to be afraid because it knows "someone" sitting out there is ready to criticize me. My crocodile reaction makes me want to run away.

One day, at the beginning of one of my presentations, I decided to experiment with my crocodile's incorrect interpretation of the situation. I confessed to the audience that, since my mother was always critical of me, it would help me a great deal if they smiled, so I'd know they were my friends. They smiled and laughed. My crocodile relaxed and then my owl was in charge. It has been successful every time both as an example of what I am talking about here and in making me more comfortable speaking to an audience.

Sometimes in relationship, you may react to your partner as if they were one of your parents with whom you had a difficult relationship, instead of your actual loving partner.

When I was eight years old, the school nurse noticed that I needed glasses. My mother was very nearsighted and wore thick glasses. She hated them and took them off whenever possible. I knew that my mother believed her glasses made her look ugly and I thought that if I wore glasses, I would be ugly and my mother wouldn't love me.

To my surprise, when I finally got glasses, the entire world became sharp and focused. What a pleasure that was! Even though I could see clearly, I believed that my glasses made me ugly and less likeable to her and everyone else. So, like my mother, I developed the habit of removing my glasses whenever I could.

Then, when I was nineteen, I met my wife-to-be, Sylvia. We fell in love. We agreed to get married when I finished medical school three years later. While we

were dating, I tried not to wear my glasses. Even though my owl knew Sylvia loved me, my crocodile remained "on guard," constantly reminding me that my glasses made me ugly and that Sylvia wouldn't like me because of them. Once, at the end of a movie, Sylvia asked, "Why do you always whip off your glasses?" Even though she asked in a friendly way, my crocodile's whole scheme of trying to be acceptable had been exposed. My face contorted with what must have looked like hatred because, in that moment, I believed that I was threatened with loss of her love. It felt like my protective system was being stripped away. My **SNN** told me that I was threatened with rejection and abandonment.

Fortunately, we were able to talk about it and I was ecstatic to find out that Sylvia liked how I looked with glasses on! It turned out that Sylvia's mother wore glasses and Sylvia loved her mother deeply. After that pivotal event, I felt good about being seen in public wearing my glasses.

The crocodile's **SNN** colors how we perceive the world and the people in it. Consider the story of the man who goes into a cave with two cans of paint: orange and black. He puts a blob of orange on the wall and then draws some black lines on top of the orange blob. He looks up at the image, screams, ""Tiger, tiger!" and runs out of the cave terrified. How often do we paint our partners as tigers? How often do we paint situations as being dangerous, when they're not—the danger being only in what we think we perceive?

As you can see, *the SNN reacts to an actual event, a fantasy, an image, a memory or a dream as if they are all perceived as equally true.* What is important to remember is that thoughts about imagined situations carry the same charge as real ones; information going into the crocodile brain, being as rapid as it is, will throw the body into a fight or flight response. Clearly, my mother is not sitting in every lecture hall, and as I begin to speak, I need to rely on my owl brain to process that fact by asking myself, "Who's talking now?" Otherwise, my mind and body will react as if my mother is in the audience. Asking myself that question greatly lessens my crocodile's power, which strengthens my owl brain.

Having a strong owl brain is good because we are less likely to be operating from a place of fear. I believe that the basic "owl" nature of most humans is that of love. We don't have to do anything to experience this love except to lessen our perception of danger that leads to fear. Love and fear are inversely related to each other.

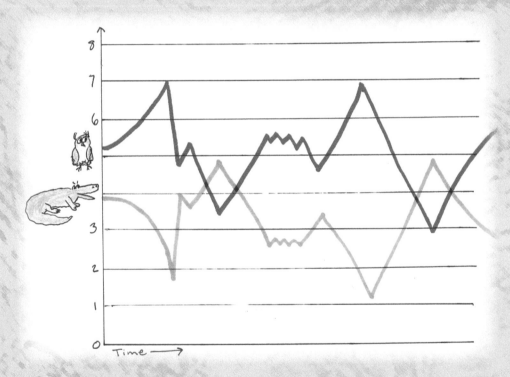

The more frightened we are, the less love we are able to bring to the relationships. Think of the sun as representing our loving nature. We don't have to turn the sun on; we only have to get rid of the clouds of fear and negativity in order to have it shine through. When your crocodile is talking, your love will be clouded by scary, negative, and angry thoughts. When the owl is talking, the voice that comes through you will be caring, positive, and sunny. Being clear about "Who's Talking Now—The Owl or The Crocodile?" allows you to disregard the impulsive, perhaps destructive nature of your crocodile and empower your "wise owl" on behalf of a happier relationship.

In the next chapter, we'll look at the tools, methods, and strategies that I have found useful in helping couples heal their relationships.

Chapter 2

WHO'S TALKING NOW? USEFUL TOOLS

Becoming aware of who is controlling what you say -- your owl or crocodile -- is probably the single most important step you can take to start the healing process which will lead to a happier relationship.

Using the strategies which I recommend in this book will help your owl become stronger and help you recognize, as early as possible, what your crocodile is feeling. You will see the crocodile's fear system with its anger and fight/flight ways as it is beginning to react. The crocodile is even willing to cause hurt and pain, including being alone (divorce), in order to guarantee its survival.

Although we can only control our own responses, if you want an empathetic, caring response from your partner, it is crucial that you not push his or her survival brain into a fight/flight way of reacting. This happens when you knowingly or unknowingly speak with blame or criticism. Instead, try using the techniques in this chapter to improve your responses and enable your partner to be on your side.

How to Recognize "Who's Talking Now?"

The moment you experience any negative feelings, such as annoyance or anger, immediately ask yourself, "Owl or Crocodile; who's talking now?"

At the moment you ask yourself the question, "Who's talking now?" you begin to rescue the situation. Your goal should be to shorten the time between when you first have the angry feeling and when you ask, "Who's talking now?" By asking this question, you slow down the whole process, giving your owl a chance to provide a thoughtful and caring response. This is going to take practice. Be patient with yourself even if you sometimes forget to ask until you are well into an argument.

What *really* is bothering you?

In my approach to healing relationships, I feel that it is crucial to get at what is *really* upsetting to you. Once you begin to notice your abrupt crocodile reactions, you may understand why your angry responses are often out of proportion to the "supposed" offense. I believe this is because underlying the anger is our crocodile's fear of danger, which it feels may ultimately lead to death. This was affirmed for me in 2000 when I read in <u>The Feeling of What Happens</u>, by Dr. Antonio Damasio[1], that we develop negative emotions as part of a warning system to alert us to the impending possibility of death.

In order to recognize the fear of death that these negative feelings represent and interrupt them from activating the crocodile, I developed the following inquiry:

· Think of an event that makes you feel angry.
· Be aware of the first thought that comes to mind after you ask yourself the question: ***Why would it bother me?***

This question can get directly to your crocodile's primitive thinking. The question can reveal the early life fears triggered by some physical and/or emotional trauma imprinted on the **SNN** of your crocodile. The "**Why would it bother you**?" process is very important because it helps your owl become aware of your crocodile's fears.

Name That Feeling

Tell your partner that you are upset. It is important that you explain your feelings in a non-accusative manner. For example, you might say, "I feel worried about being late and I am frightened that the Joneses will not like me if we arrive late to the party." This is better than the blaming accusation, "Because of you, we are going to be late."

I have introduced you to what I believe underlies all angry arguments. Confrontations of all kinds are common in relationships. Now I will present some tools to use to make these confrontations friendlier.

Useful Tools:

Compliment before Challenging--
How to Avoid Provoking Your Partner's (or Anyone Else's) Crocodile

An unfriendly atmosphere between couples invites the crocodiles to come out and take over the discussion. Remember that in the rush to survive, a crocodile often misinterprets the actions or words of another person as a death threat.

Here is a simple idea that can help when you are anticipating a challenging conversation, and that can then lead to a positive outcome.

Begin by saying something complimentary to your partner *before* you get to the difficult part of your discussion. For example, "That's a pretty blouse that you're wearing. You look great today! I heard that you got a promotion at work - congratulations!" Actually, the lighter and more fun-loving you can be, the more effective it can be in establishing a friendly atmosphere! (Wise owls have a gentle sense of humor while crocodiles have none.)

Most couples figure out a style which works for them. The more sincere the compliments are, the better. For example, a single word such as "sweetie," a gentle touch, or a smile creates friendliness. By starting this way, you are inviting cooperation between both of your owls to prevent agitating each other's crocodiles.

Ask For Help

For many people, asking for help can be scary because it reveals vulnerability. However, asking for help can actually lead to greater intimacy because it involves activating compassion and empathy in each partner. Asking for help acknowledges and strengthens the interdependence of the relationship.

As simple as it sounds, saying something like "Please help me" can be difficult, yet quite effective. Saying "please" will empower the other person, who might otherwise have felt threatened. For example, you might say, "Honey, I so enjoy watching movies with you. Would you please help with the dishes while I get the kids to bed, so that later we can watch together?"

Take Responsibility and Apologize

Working with these tools is an ongoing process. No matter how adept you become at recognizing your crocodile and using these techniques, from time to time your crocodile may sneak out and cause you to say or do hurtful things. In general, we are not aware of the brief unintended facial expressions that we make or the harsh voice tones that we use. These reactions send implicit messages which are received by, and cause pain to, the other person. It is crucial to be able to take responsibility and apologize for

knowingly or unknowingly causing another person pain.

In addition, it's important how you frame your apology. In other words, just saying, "I'm sorry that you were pained by my comment" does not soothe the other person's crocodile fears. A more skillful way of saying this would be, "I'm sorry that *I* caused you pain." This is a direct, clear statement and puts the responsibility where it should be, on you.

The seven chapters that follow present ordinary people with everyday problems who were unable to make their relationships work due to the hyperactivity of their crocodiles. As you read, notice the ways in which your problems are similar to those described, helping you become aware of your own crocodile. You might recognize your own impulse to pout, fight, or run away.

It is my hope that these stories will provide useful examples of how the tools can be used to improve difficult relationships. You will see how an owl which is truly awake and in charge can allow a relationship to flourish.

Chapter 3

COFFEE ON THE CROTCH

Description of the Couple

Larry, a man in his mid-thirties, appeared more worried than his slightly younger, very thin wife, Carol. At first his facial muscles were tense as he looked around my office. I thought he might be bothered by the piles of papers on my desk, since he continued to stare at them. He frequently checked his watch. I learned that Larry was in charge of the service department of a Porsche dealership. He was proud that his area was so clean that "you could eat off the floor." His casual pants and shirt were carefully starched and pressed.

Carol seemed to be trying to be nice. She said all of the right introductory things but they seemed absent of feelings. Her smile was forced and stiff. I thought her choice of clothing and her hairstyle gave her a waif-like appearance. She said her work as a lab technician was gratifying because it gave her the opportunity to make many friends.

The Problem

Carol and Larry came to see me because the problems in their ten-year-old marriage were causing them to think of separating. They had three daughters, ages three, five and eight. They were frightened that the love they once had for each other was fading. Their fights centered on Carol being angry that Larry was not available for her needs. Larry was upset because Carol was always nagging him to spend more time with her, leaving him no time at all for any of his other interests.

In their marriage, Larry and Carol acted with each other in the same ways they had learned to cope as children. Carol played the "good girl" but on occasion exploded with rage like her mother. Larry switched back and forth between giving angry orders and criticizing Carol, and then pouting until he felt he had permission to go off on his own.

Background

    Carol, the youngest of six children, was raised in an upper middle-class Catholic family. Her father was a wealthy real estate developer. Her mother was quick to anger and, according to Carol, "was exhausted all of the time." Thus, Carol did not get much nurturing and, in fact, ended up taking care of her mother. Her way to avoid her mother's anger was to always try to act the way she was supposed to. She learned to be quiet and make no demands.

    Her brothers and sisters were also emotionally deprived and would frequently beat Carol because they were jealous of whatever attention their mother gave her. Confrontation, anger and rage were the norm in her childhood home. Her father provided little comfort, as he was often away working.

Larry was the older of two boys raised in a middle-class working family. His father had trained front-line troops in the Marines. After retiring he ran a small contracting company and treated his family in an authoritative and harsh way as if they were a Marine platoon. That frightened Larry's older brother and their mother. Larry avoided his father by being away from home as much as possible, often going fishing with friends.

The Session

Dr. B: In order for me to help you see how my approach works with your everyday marital problems, I would like one of you to tell me about a recent disagreement so that we all can look at it together.

Larry: Okay, I've got one. Last night Carol and I were dressing to go to a party. I told her that she looked beautiful and sexy and that after we came back from the party we could make love. Carol got furious with me and accused me of only being interested in her for sex. She was waving her arms wildly and knocked over a cup of hot coffee that was sitting on the table onto the front of my pants. I was in a lot of pain and I started

to scream that she was a mean bitch. She screamed back at me that I was a selfish, inconsiderate bastard who wanted sex all of the time.

Dr. B: Wow, this sounds like this was more than just a small disagreement! Okay, let's use what happened to help you both see that behind the surface upset there was a deep set of fears. These fears drive our crocodiles to respond thirty times faster than our slower and wiser owl brains. I would like to start by talking to these crocodile brains. Answer the questions I ask with whatever comes to mind first. Just give it a try, okay? Carol, I'll begin with you. Who do you think was talking in you when you screamed at Larry that "he was a selfish inconsiderate bastard who wanted sex all of the time?"

Carol: When you put it that way, I would have to say it was my crocodile.

Dr. B: And **why would it bother you** if Larry wants sex all the time?

Carol: Because that would mean that he didn't see me as a person with my own needs.

Dr. B: **Why would it bother you** if he didn't see you as a person with your own needs?

Carol: That's what I had growing up—nobody was interested in my needs.

Dr. B: **Why would it bother you** if no one was interested in your needs?

Carol: There would be nobody to take care of me.

Dr. B: **Why would it bother you** if no one took care of you?

Carol: I wouldn't survive. I would die.

Larry reaches out to comfort Carol by squeezing her arm lightly. It is quiet for a few moments. I wait for Larry and Carol to recover and the new insights sink in.

Dr. B: So Carol, you can see how the Supersensitive Neural Network of your crocodile is hypersensitive. It misperceived the present and interpreted what was happening as if you were still in your childhood.

Dr. B: Now Larry, first I'd like to ask you who was talking in you when you were screaming at Carol.

Larry: Yup, it was my crocodile.

Dr. B: I'd like to help you see if there is anything useful you can find under your anger. **Why would it bother you** to get hot coffee poured on your suit?

Larry: Wouldn't it bother anyone?

Dr. B: Of course, but why did it bother *you*?

Larry: It might not be possible to clean the suit pants well, and besides the coffee was hot and she spilled it in my lap.

Dr. B: Aside from the pain and heat, **why would it bother you**?

Larry: Because it was so unfair.

Dr. B: **Why would it bother you** if someone was unfair to you?

Larry: Wouldn't it bother anybody?

Dr. B: Yes, of course, but **why would it bother you**?

Larry: [His eyes well up with tears] I just had a memory of when I was a child. My father suddenly turned on me and started to holler and beat me

without any reason. He was very powerful physically, and I thought that he would kill me.

Dr. B: I'd like you both to recognize how you see each other through your early life experiences - Carol, with your mother, and Larry, with your father. The very fast crocodile brain, whose job it is to protect you, reacts automatically and causes you to think and feel as you did when you were much younger.

Everyone thinks and feels in ways that reflect their early life experiences. People who were hurt emotionally or physically early in life, who did not experience empathy from their parents, have a hard time developing their owl brain. Their crocodile brains say, "Only my hurts are important." It is understandable that they would have a difficult time recognizing their partner's needs.

Now, let's use this understanding to revisit the hot coffee fight. Use your own style, of course, but have your owls control the process. Okay? Carol, why don't you go first?

Carol: When you said, "Let's have sex after the party," I got furious. I've always assumed that you only care for me because of what I do sexually for you—never for myself.

Larry's face begins to contort when he hears Carol's words.

Dr. B: Carol, do you see how Larry was looking daggers at you when you just said that?

Larry: Well, sure. It wasn't fair. I am a caring person and you are mean to say those things. You make me feel terrible when you say that.

Dr. B: Can you both see how you are blaming each other and saying "You are bad?" This will usually start another crocodile fight, because they will fight to the death to be right. The crocodile believes that only "right" people are loved. "Wrong" people are rejected. This then activates the primitive fear of not surviving. If one of you is right and the other wrong, you will both lose. Try to remember that there is only one issue on the table: how are we going to make this into a win-win. Carol, why don't you give it a try again, being careful not to use any language which could be perceived as blaming?

Carol: When I tried "**Why would it bother you**?" it came out that I was really afraid of dying. I know you are a very good person and a superb dad. I would really appreciate if you would help me with my fear that I am not worth anything to you except for my body. Please help me with this fear. I feel terrible about burning you with hot coffee. Forgive me for doing that. I just lost control. I understand now that you were just trying to connect with me.

Larry's face softens as he listens to Carol.

Dr. B: Larry, why don't you give it a try now?

Larry: Okay. Carol, even though you didn't bring it up directly, I want to apologize for ignoring you so often when I'm doing my hobbies. Maybe it's no wonder that you think that I just like you for sex. Also, when the hot coffee got poured on my crotch I got scared. I lost it, and called you some mean names. I'm sorry my screaming scared you so. Thinking back, I realize I was scared too, just like when my dad told me I was selfish and then beat me to within an inch of my life. I was afraid that I would die from Dad and also from you. Honey, please help me with this one—it's big for me.

And while I'm at it, I want to apologize for how I nitpick if the house isn't perfectly neat and fine like my auto-shop. I really *do* know that with three children that's almost impossible.

Carol smiles gently and reaches for Larry's hand...

The Healing

As Larry and Carol practiced these techniques every time they had a fight, trust grew. They acknowledged the difficulties that each had had growing up and had more compassion for each other. They became more affectionate, appreciating each other's strengths and weaknesses. They adapted, shortened and modified my approach to fit their own styles and words. Their relationship has strengthened as they look forward to raising their children, taking vacations together, and developing their own musical and athletic interests.

Comments to the Reader

It is interesting to see what an incredible opportunity marriage provides to rework our childhood problems and see our partner through our most mature eyes.

Here we see Carol adopting a more helpless style, inviting Larry to care for her, which he does, but not with a lot of empathy. He adopts his father's style of coping, which was always being in control, or reverting to his childhood's style of running away.

In both we see the different ways of expressing the fight/flight reaction to the underlying survival fears.

Chapter 5

THE TWO "MAD" RUSSIANS

Description of the Couple

Boris and Natasha, both in their mid-forties, came to see me on a hot summer day. Boris was in shorts and sneakers while Natasha was attired in more elegant clothing. Initially it was Boris who did all of the talking, with Natasha making faces when she didn't agree with him. They reminded me of two animals waiting to pounce on each other. As the hour went on, Natasha attacked Boris several times with a raised voice and sarcastic comments. Boris did not express his negative feelings, but his face became beet red. At one point in the session Natasha threatened to leave the room if Boris continued to say "those things" about her. When I asked what specific remarks upset her, it turned out to be more Boris's tone of voice and harsh facial contortions than what he actually said.

Natasha also complained about how hard she had to work in order to help with the family finances and how she resented having to deal with customers in the dress shop in which she was a sales person for a few hours a day. In contrast, Boris and Natasha glowed with pride when describing their eight-year-old twin boys and the home they had built over ten years where they could nurture and raise them. Boris enjoyed nature and was very pleased to tell me how well he managed a local garden shop.

The Problem

Initially, Boris and Natasha were unclear as to why they phoned for an appointment, saying that they had heard that I was helpful with the problems that couples have, and that they wanted to make their marriage better. But, once they began to talk to me, it became clear from their facial gestures, voice tone, and body language that there were fires burning just beneath the surface. Natasha said that Boris didn't respect her and was always ordering her around. She further complained that when Boris ordered her around he did so with harsh voice and a "mean face." Boris's complaint was that no matter how hard he worked and tried to make a good home for his family, it was never good enough for Natasha, and that she screamed at him and the children.

Background

Natasha came from a rigidly orthodox Jewish family that had emigrated from Russia. Her parents related poorly to her and to each other. Natasha described her mother as "screaming at me constantly and finding fault with everything I did." Her father, a traveling salesman, was away from home frequently and, by Natasha's account, not interested in her or her older brother. When Natasha was thirteen, her parents divorced and Natasha stayed with her mother.

Boris, also of Russian origin, was the eldest of four children. He was given the job of helping to raise his sister and brothers. The saving grace for Boris was that his mother was very loving to him. His father criticized him and said that Boris was not as capable or as smart as he himself was. Boris felt that his mother always sided with him and that this made his

father jealous. It seemed to me that Boris had taken on the generosity and kindness of his mother as well as the harsh critical style and stern face of his father.

The Session

Dr. B: I want to help you both recognize what it is that gets so activated in the day to day activities of your marriage and explore who is really talking. Let's start with you, Natasha. You said that the main thing that upsets you about Boris is his meanness as shown by his harsh voice and face. **Why would it bother you** if he makes a mean face and speaks in a harsh voice?

Natasha: I feel that he is telling me that I am a bad person.

Dr. B: **Why would it bother you** if he tells you that you are a bad person?

Natasha: If I am a bad girl that means that no one will like me.

Dr. B: **Why would it bother you** if no one likes you?

Natasha: If no one likes me then I won't have any friends and I'll be alone.

Dr. B: **Why would it bother you** if you are alone?

Natasha: I don't think that I could survive. As I was growing up my mother was always there, screaming at me. It seemed to me that she hated me so much and I constantly worried that she would leave me or get rid of me like my father did. I realize now that I was so frightened that I did everything I could to take care of her so that she would need me and wouldn't desert me. I guess this is why I never felt that anyone cared about my needs or wants.

Natasha's hands are trembling and tears are welling up in her eyes. Boris reaches out and gives her forearm a reassuring squeeze.

Dr. B: Boris, since you already see where this is all going, try to focus on my questions and respond with the first thing that comes to mind, even if it doesn't make sense. I want to hear what your crocodile thinks about these matters. You said that you didn't like Natasha complaining that you were not doing well enough. **Why would it bother you**?

Boris: I don't like being told time and time again that I am not doing things the right way.

Dr. B: **Why would it bother you** if you don't do things "in the right way?"

Boris: I pride myself in what I do. That is who I am. If my most important person, my wife, feels I'm doing badly, then I feel unloveable, even though I should be loved.

Dr. B: **Why would it bother you** if you are not loveable?

Boris: I guess I would feel what Natasha felt. As I grew up, my friends loved me, my mother and siblings loved me, but not my father. I am still trying to get my father to love and respect me.

Dr. B: Natasha, it sounds like you married someone who reminds you of the harshness and meanness of your mother. And I guess Boris feels that you resemble his father in how you respond to him. People often unconsciously recreate situations from their childhood in their own adult relationships. Perhaps this happens because it is the only way of being in a relationship that they know. Both of you really hope to be cared for in a kind and respectful way. You both deserve to get those good things you want. Let's figure out how to break the old cycles and emerge with better and more loving endings.

The goal is to have your owl be in charge while not threatening your partner's crocodile. Remember, you want to help your partner stay in their owl brain for a win-win ending. With your owls in charge, you can talk to each other in a way that isn't hurtful.

Boris, why don't you give it a try using the problems you both mentioned earlier. Remember, if it's not a win-win, it's a lose-lose. And please be patient with yourself and your partner since it probably took a lifetime to develop your unskillful ways of handling relationships. It takes time and practice to get it right.

Boris: Natasha, I get so mad when you don't appreciate anything I do for you and the kids. It just frosts me! First my father and then you.

Dr. B: Can you see how your Supersensitive Neural Network set you up to be hyper-reactive to this situation? In its speed to react to what it perceived as a threat, it confused Natasha with your dad. Boris, everything you said may be truthful and accurate, but can you think of another way to say it that does not frighten Natasha? Try to remember that for a win-win to occur, the owls have to come out and the crocodiles stay asleep. Why don't you try it again, keeping in mind this approach?

Boris: Okay. Before I even start, I want to apologize for making a mean face and saying things in a nasty way. My father did that all the time and I hated it. I can't see my face, but I'll take your word for it. I got furious that you felt I wasn't doing enough and that you yelled at me. After doing the **"Why would it bother you**?" method, though, I know that at some crocodile level I felt that my life was in danger. You are the greatest cuddler in the world when I don't upset you. And when I don't forget, I know how much you go out of your way to help me feel important. Also, if I don't frighten you, you listen and pay attention to what I say and stay affectionate with me. That means so much! So Natasha, please help me so that I don't get so scared like I used to with my father.

Dr. B: Great! Natasha, why don't you give it a try?

Natasha: Boris, when you yell and make faces at me, I feel just like when my mother slapped me on the face and ordered me around. I knew for sure that she had no respect for me. I got enraged at you just like I got enraged at her. I think that what I was really upset about is my fear that you are going to leave me. I got frightened that I wouldn't be able to survive on my own.

Dr. B: You both did great! You acknowledged that you have been angry, but afterwards you realized that it was your frightened crocodile that had responded and not your wise owl. Crocodiles are particularly threatened by being told they are bad. In response they come out and say something like, "Oh yeah, you're really the bad one, not me, because you started it." Then the fight's on between the two crocodiles.

Natasha: Okay, Boris, you are quite right that I can be sarcastic and mean when I say that you don't do enough and that you are a bad father and husband. I know that you are a good husband and father and I apologize for hurting you. You are very helpful with little things around the house, stuff that my parents always made me do like taking out the garbage, walking the dogs, and cleaning up their messes. I know that you do these things to make my life easier, and when I'm thinking straight, you are the greatest husband! Please help me with my fear of angry faces. Maybe we can work out some system where I can let you know – but not in a nasty way – that you're making faces.

Dr. B: Wonderful. I want both of you to keep in mind that it's very important to practice these techniques at home when I am not there so that you can become more skilled at this.

The Healing

After practicing these new approaches they eventually stopped the pouting and shouting. In time Natasha became more aware of how much she had unknowingly taken on her mother's negative traits and Boris became more aware of how often he spoke with the same harshness as his father.

This resulted in their beginning to feel greater trust in the relationship. Boris could see that if he did the same things he did before, but with a different voice and facial expression, Natasha was happy and responsive to him. When Natasha said things that showed a sense of entitlement and self-centeredness, Boris could *gently* talk to her about it and help her to see how much more affection she would get from him when she spoke from her owl. The children, who had previously witnessed their parents' fighting, became much more lighthearted due to the greater sense of security at home.

Comments to the Reader

Here we see how Natasha was saying to Boris all of the things that she, as a child, was frightened to say to her mother. For instance, she would say to Boris that he was not doing enough to take care of her. In this case she was really talking about her mother.

And then Boris, because of his own fears, reacted by attacking with his voice and facial expressions. He becomes more like Natasha's childhood mother.

The compulsion to "repeat" the past in order to now "fix" it is evident here. Now their childhood scenarios are resurrected, and unless the current approaches are changed, those old childhood endings take place, leading to feelings of rejection and pain.

Chapter 6

PIZZA IN VENICE

Description of the Couple

Tom and Theresa were in their early sixties. They arrived dressed neatly but casually. Tom seemed a bit hesitant, and looked down on the ground a lot as if he were depressed. Theresa looked directly at me, and had a radiant smile.

This was the first time that they had ever seen a therapist and both were a bit nervous. Theresa was clearly the more talkative of the two. Tom, jaw muscles clenched and face frowning, appeared to be angry while listening to her view of their problems. They both told me about their long-term marriage, their three children and five grandchildren. Theresa was still working very happily as a second grade teacher, while Tom worked as a piano tuner and amateur musician.

The Problem

When I asked them to tell me about the problems that brought them to me, Theresa began telling me what had happened when they went to Venice to celebrate their last anniversary. She said it illustrated the upsets that they had had with each other.

Theresa remembered enough of the Italian that was spoken in her childhood home to be the translator on their trip. At a restaurant one evening, Tom wanted to order a pizza with different ingredients than those listed on the menu. Theresa was annoyed at Tom and didn't want to order it for him. Theresa said that she didn't want to bother the waiter, who already appeared to be harried and impatient. Tom got angry because he felt that she cared more about the waiter's feelings than about his. This was typical of many of the fights that plagued their marriage.

Background

Tom's mother died in childbirth, and for the first few years of his life he was in several foster homes because his father, a day laborer, was unable to take care of him. When Tom was two years old, his father re-married. Tom remembers his stepmother as a bitter, hypercritical woman, who resented him from the beginning. She often beat Tom, and blamed his father for making her life so difficult. Today Tom frequently

worries about having enough money, food, and security. I think that these fears had their origin in his early emotional abuse.

Theresa was raised by very loving Italian parents and grandparents and always felt that she would be cared for. She was also concerned, as her parents and grandparents had been, with how her actions would make others feel. As a child her parents instilled in her the importance of putting others' feelings and needs ahead of her own.

The Session

Dr. B: Before we can actually solve the problem, it will be very important to learn what is behind the bickering and fighting; these are just the surface symptoms, and not the underlying problem. In order to do this I need to have a talk with your crocodile brains. I'll ask you a question, and to the best of your ability, try to answer it spontaneously. Tell me the first thing that comes to your mind. Okay, Tom, why don't we start with you?

Tom: Okay.

Dr. B: **Why would it bother you** if Theresa didn't want to ask the waiter to get different things for your pizza?

Tom: It would mean that she didn't care about my needs.

Dr. B: Please forget for a moment that the question sounds stupid, but **why would it bother you** if she didn't care about your needs?

Tom: As I was growing up, I never felt anyone cared for my needs. One of the reasons that I married Theresa was that she was such a loving person. If she didn't care about my needs, then I would be all alone again emotionally, like when I was a kid.

Dr. B: **Why would it bother you** to be emotionally alone again?

Tom: If nobody cared about my needs, then it would be me struggling to survive. As a kid I could never relax. When I look back now I can see how I was always preparing for the worst.

Dr. B: So **why would it bother you** to be alone and struggling to survive?

Tom: I get so tired struggling, and if I didn't feel anyone was with me emotionally, then I don't think that I could survive.

Theresa, moved by how the pizza episode triggered a childhood fear of not surviving, reached out and caressed Tom's arm.

Dr. B: That was very helpful, Tom. Now Theresa, let's see if there is anything more to the fight you were having with Tom. **why would it bother you** if Tom asked you to have the waiter change the ingredients for the pizza?

Theresa: I felt that the waiter was annoyed and that he was probably having a hard day. I didn't want to burden him with any extra problems.

Dr. B: **Why would it bother you** to burden the waiter with an extra problem?

Theresa: That's the way I was brought up. If my mother were here, she would agree with me. You try not to cause other people problems!

Dr. B: So if your mother was here, **why would it bother you** if she saw you causing others problems?

Theresa: She would be disappointed in me.

Dr. B: And **why would it bother you** if she were disappointed in you?

Theresa: That would mean that she would love me less. As I now think about it, I know she would actually understand and not love me less. But I guess some part of me, probably my crocodile, thinks it.

Dr. B: Try to stay with your crocodile thinking. **Why would it bother you** if she loved you less?

Theresa: I watched where Tom went with this, and I guess I can see how some part of me would feel threatened. But I don't ever remember feeling a threat to my survival.

Dr. B: Theresa, even considering intellectually the possibility that some part of you would feel threatened might be enough for you to try to use the repair process that I describe. Now that you have the idea that behind all negative feelings and thoughts lies some crocodile fears about survival, let's go on to the repair process. Remember to keep asking yourselves, "Would you rather be happy or right?" Unfortunately, we often choose to be right. If it isn't win-win, then it will be lose-lose. Okay, Theresa, why don't you try using the Venice pizza story and see if you can come to a win-win ending.

Theresa: Honey, I really do love you. When you asked me to get the waiter to put other ingredients in the pizza, I could see that he was already impatient and annoyed. I got caught in a double bind: I was brought up to not upset others, and at the same time, I wanted to please you too. I guess I assumed that you know how much I care for you. So first I got annoyed at you, and then I realized that I was afraid that you wouldn't like me and that the waiter would be irritated at me and he wouldn't like me either. I just need to tell you that when you get unhappy with me your face gets contorted and I worry that you will hit me, just like your stepmother hit you. I know you won't, but I get scared of you anyway.

Dr. B: It's great that you could notice all of the subtleties of Tom's face and body language. You were probably accurate. But for our purposes here, in order to get to a win-win, it would be helpful to let Tom know that you are frightened without implying that he is bad like his stepmother. Since she frequently told him that he was bad, he will probably hear you as putting him down and not liking him. When he gets frightened, his crocodile comes out. It doesn't hear you and wants to bite you. Maybe leave out the part about how he looks like his mean stepmother.

Theresa: I think I understand that. Tom, you are really such a thoughtful husband and take such good care of my needs that I guess I assumed that my not wanting to ask the waiter would be okay with you. Please forgive me for hurting your feelings. I would appreciate your help with the double-bind I got into between your needs and the waiter's needs. I guess I get worried that somebody won't like me. For now, could you please rescue me?

Theresa is smiling playfully and Tom responds by touching her cheek gently.

Dr. B: Great. Now Tom, it's your turn.

Tom: Just hearing you talk that way makes me feel good. Thank you. I know I get scared easily. It's a problem I have and I do need to work on it. When

I hear anything that sounds like, or I can interpret as, "I don't care about your needs," I get enraged inside, and then I hate you, and I think that you are mean and cruel and I wonder how you could be doing this to me.

Dr. B: Here again we can see your previously traumatized **SNN** reacting to Theresa as if she were your mother. Even if Theresa is being insensitive at the time, there is no constructive purpose in commenting on that, since her crocodile will then come out in response to what she sees as a threat—either from displeasing the waiter or you. In any case, that comment doesn't lead to a win-win ending. Just let her know that you are frightened. I'm aware that this is hard to do. But with practice it gets easier.

Tom: I know from the **"Why would it bother you**?" question that I'm terrified about my survival. I've had this for my entire life. I married you because of your kindness. I wish I could be that way, so that I could think more gently, but I'm not there yet. In the meantime, could you please help me, so even when you don't want to do what I ask, just tell me in some way that you still like me. I know that I have to do more of the work. Hopefully, my need for so much reassurance will be temporary. I feel terrible that I hurt the person that I love the most. I know that I do it less than before, but I still feel awful for upsetting you and probably causing most of our disagreements.

The Healing

When they got married, Tom and Theresa made the commitment to be together "until death do us part" and they meant to keep that vow. They hoped counseling would end the bickering between them that had become habitual. What developed as a result of their learning was greater ease and sweetness between them. There were more episodes of tender connection and deeper conversations with less likelihood of one or the other becoming upset. They began to talk of their retirement years and how they would like to spend them together. An awareness of the frailty of life, with the death and sickness of friends and relatives, permitted them to use their time together in a satisfying way, rather than wasting it with bickering and fighting. They were also pleasantly surprised to find that they could teach their grandchildren to use the concepts of the owl and the crocodile with good results.

Comments to the Reader

In this story we see how the problems of our childhood are remembered throughout our entire life by our crocodile. Our crocodile may eventually use more complex words and actions, but emotionally it never grows up and frequently responds in its most infantile and unwise ways. Our owl matures over time and is able to deal more wisely with the complex stresses which occur in everyday life.

Tom's lifelong fear of abandonment revealed itself with his hyper-sensitivity to anything Theresa said, which he could interpret as insensitivity to his needs. Just as a frightened baby is not aware of the needs of its mother, Tom was not aware of the needs of Theresa during these episodes.

Chapter 7

ATTILA AND THE MAIDEN

Description of the Couple

In their early 30's, Barry and Mary were a strikingly handsome couple. Barry looked and walked like a football linebacker approaching the scrimmage line. After graduating from college, he had been a semiprofessional wrestler for a number of years and was now the part owner of a small gymnasium. Mary was tentative and shy, seeming to defer to Barry. Her style worked well in her job as executive secretary in a large company.

They usually came to their appointment after work. Barry wore jeans, running shoes, and tight T-shirts that revealed his muscular body. It seemed to me that Mary, an attractive woman, dressed in a haphazard way as if she needed a "mommy" to make the most of her good looks.

The Problem

Before they got married, Barry lived on the west coast of the United States, while Mary lived on the east coast. The continent that separated them made it possible to avoid the many problems that would have occurred had they lived closer. Now that they lived together, Barry complained that Mary was lazy and wasn't doing enough to make their home comfortable and warm for his needs. Mary said that he criticized her frequently with a contorted angry face and a booming, commanding voice. This really frightened her. She would then retaliate by withdrawing and withholding the positive support that he wanted. Barry was the "fighter" and Mary, by pouting, was the "fleer."

Their Background

Both Barry and Mary had parents with substantial emotional problems. All four parents chronically abused alcohol and had been divorced several times. Mary was the oldest of six children while Barry was an only child. His father, now a retired dentist, often had rage attacks and was physically violent with his young son. Barry described his mother as silly, like a baby.

Mary's parents were fundamentally affectionate and caring, but both of them struggled with alcoholism. During periods when they were drunk, Mary had to take care of them.

The Session

Dr. B: Today let's look at how your crocodiles are trying to hurt or even destroy the closeness you have now. The crocodile agenda is safety and survival, not love and closeness. I want you to see what your crocodile is feeling when your fights first begin. Try to say the first thing that comes to your mind after I ask the questions.

Barry, why don't we start with you? **Why would it bother you** if Mary is lazy and doesn't do enough to make your home warm and comfortable?

Barry: That means to me that she doesn't care for me.

Dr. B: **Why would it bother you** if she doesn't care for you?

Barry: Look, I'm in this marriage for life and if I'm never going to get cared for it will feel like being all alone again, like I was my whole life. There would be no one I could depend on.

His voice quivers, and then gets tight and angry.

Dr. B: **Why would it bother you** if you were all alone again?

Barry: I know this sounds stupid, because I am very able to take of myself, yet
at some level I have always felt that I wouldn't make it. When my father
was beating on me as a kid, I never felt that I had anyone to protect
or care for me. I was sure he hated me. My mother was never around,
and there were no older sisters or brothers to take my side. I became a
wrestler to prevent anyone from messing with me. When I met Mary, I
felt for sure that she was the one person in my life who would love me
and take care of me. I hate it that when I get upset, I become just like my
father who was so hateful when he screamed at me.

Dr. B: I understand. Sometimes we behave like a parent who frightened us
so we can feel that we are in control of the situation. Mary, I'd like
to approach this a little differently for you and not focus on Barry's
contorted face and harsh voice, but rather on some other aspect of your
problem with him. Your work and school history certainly shows that
you are not a lazy person. I think you'd agree that wanting a warm,
caring home is not unreasonable. **Why would it bother you** to make a
reasonable effort in this area?

At this point Mary looks puzzled.

Mary: I never thought of this until now, but I feel as if I was cheated as a
kid. I always had to take care of my brothers and sisters as well as my
parents. Nobody ever took care of me. When I met Barry, I really thought
that he would love me no matter what and that he would take care of all
of *my* needs. I know this sounds crazy, but I feel entitled to get cared for
without my having to do anything!

Dr. B: Mary, you are right. You did get cheated. When you were very young,
you were entitled to be cared for without having to do anything. Would
it bother you to know that you can only get that kind of unlimited care
when you are young?

Mary looks very sad and begins to cry.

Mary: It's not fair! I know that I have been demanding this from Barry, but a part of me feels that if I don't get my needs met without having to do anything, then I don't have a chance of surviving.

Barry leans forward and touches Mary's arm.

Barry: Sweetie, we have to figure this out, otherwise how will we be able to have children and raise them right?

Dr. B: I want to compliment both of you for your efforts to bring these crocodiles to the surface. This is how you are allowing your wiser and more loving owl systems be more in control. Keep in mind that your negative ways of relating are lifelong habits and may well take a long time to be resolved. A sign of success in this work is that you spend less time annoyed at each other.

Now I would like to have you practice using your own words to fix the "Mary is lazy and Barry is ferocious and angry" issue. Our goal is to "regroove" the nerve pathways in the brain so that you will automatically do what is owl-skillful and break the crocodile cycle of hurt and revenge. Try it as if you are at home and speaking to each other.

Barry: I know I got freaked out because when I came home from work on Sunday, the dirty dishes were piled up in the sink and you were watching TV. I got angry at you for being so lazy while I work so hard. When I calmed down a little and I asked myself why these piled up dishes bothered me, I remembered how my whole life I wasn't taken care of and felt that I wouldn't make it.

Dr. B: Barry, how are you going to get Mary to help you if you tell her that she is lazy? That will frighten her and just lead to both of your crocodiles fighting.

Barry is deep in thought for several moments.

Barry: I keep forgetting to make friends with you first. So, here goes. Mary, you load the dishwasher so much better than I do and you look so pretty today.

Mary begins to smile since she knows what is coming. But it's working. Then Barry smiles too. (Crocodiles never smile!)

Barry: Mary, first I want to apologize for calling you lazy. I saw the dishes in the sink and I got angry, but then I recognized where that came from. I realized that I worry that I am not loveable. Mary, please help me with this.

Mary: Barry, I do love you, you kook! This laziness thing is something that I have to work out with the little me. I'm sorry you have to deal with the result. I guess I'm hoping that you will be the good Mom that I never had. I am sorry. Could you please help me and us both, like you did today? You didn't scream and shoot daggers at me from your eyes. You reminded me that you were in pain. That helped so much. I will really try to make a greater effort in the future. I know that when I am screamed at, I feel like a little girl in my parents' home. I get terrified and want to run away.

Barry: Mary, just before when you said "I love you, you kook!" it was like magic for me. I am also sorry for my frequent barking and scaring you. I want for us to have children someday and I know that if I ever yell at our kids like I have at you, I'll hate myself. I have to stop my nasty and angry comments. I can't see my face when I'm screaming at you. I hope that you point that out to me kindly when I look scary to you. I know this is asking you to do something very hard.

Mary: I think the fact that we both are trying to be softer, gentler and non-guilt tripping will help us greatly. At least it will me. If at least one of us can stay cool and not angry, it will help the other calm down faster.

The Healing

Barry and Mary took several months to fully integrate this approach in all their disagreements, but they kept practicing. Barry rarely became enraged and Mary tried more and more to please Barry. Ultimately they developed a trust so that even if their crocodiles had a fight, their owls were able to work it out, sometimes even laughing at themselves.

Comments to the Reader

In this story we see how the frightened crocodile is concerned about the owl asking for help because it fears that that will make it vulnerable and appear weak. In their childhood, their parents were not trustworthy and they felt unsafe asking for help. Now as adults, when they learned it was safe to ask for help from their spouse, most often the spouse responded positively. Problems are likely to arise when the crocodile, out of fear, does not give the wise owl the opportunity to respond and ask for help in a kindly way.

Chapter 8

The Professor and the Blonde

Description of The Couple

Michael, a college Latin teacher in his mid-forties, appeared worried as he entered my office for our first interview. He was trim and neatly dressed in a suit and a bow tie. He alternated biting his cuticles, cracking his knuckles, and bouncing his legs up and down. His wife, Olivia, an attractive woman, was a few years younger than Michael. Her shrill, rather tight voice let me know that she was tense and angry. Her anger changed into periods of depression when she became quiet and looked down at the floor. She complained about her difficulties with raising their four children, who ranged in age from four to seventeen.

The Problem

Olivia and Michael came to see me because of their almost daily fighting. During their eighteen-year marriage, individual and marriage counseling brought little relief to their constant friction. They frequently considered divorce.

Olivia was aware of her "short fuse" and "hot temper." She complained that Michael had a hard time talking and was often withdrawn. Michael retorted that Olivia always needed things her way or she would be angry. Olivia leaned forward and spoke rapidly, telling Michael in a demanding way how he was wrong and how he was failing to meet her needs. Michael reacted to this by becoming downcast, nonresponsive, and sometimes appearing withdrawn with a glazed look in his eyes. At other times Michael counterattacked with sarcastic and cruel remarks.

Even with all of the above negativity, I felt that there had to have been a deep core of loving and caring in order for them to survive eighteen years of marriage.

Background

Michael described growing up with a very depressed father and a cold, demanding mother who hoped he would become "someone important so she could feel proud." Olivia grew up in a household with angry parents who often screamed at each other and at her. She said that her mother was very emotionally injured and self-centered, and that her father was away from home a lot. When he was present he was often sullen or angry.

The Session

Dr. B: Before trying to fix anything, I think that it is very important to first find out what's underneath your negative feelings. To help you do this I would like for your owls to see what the crocodiles are thinking and feeling. So when I ask you a question, try not to think about the answer, but rather just blurt out whatever is in your mind.

Michael, even though this may sound like a silly question, **why would it bother you** that Olivia tells you are wrong and that you always fail to meet her needs?

Michael: She basically keeps telling me that I am bad.

Dr. B: **Why would it bother you** to be told that you are bad?

Michael: If that is what Olivia really thinks of me, then that means that I am not loveable.

Dr. B: So **why would it bother you** if you were not loveable?

Michael: I grew up my whole life with a mother who was always interested only in her own interests. I felt that I was a bother to her. She never actually told me that I was bad, but I assumed it was true because she always looked angry, as if she didn't like me. Although I was fed and clothed, she was cold to me. I felt lonesome. To have it definitely said that I'm bad would make me fall apart and become a worthless blob of nothingness.

Dr. B: In essence you would be dead.

Michael: Yes. That's exactly what I felt most of my life—that I was dead, but still moving.

Olivia, listening to this, with widening eyes, begins to get an idea of what has been happening to Michael.
Her face softens.

Dr. B: Olivia, even though you have been listening to Michael do this, try as best you can to say the first thing that comes to mind after my question so we can find out what your crocodile is thinking rather than your logical brain.

Olivia: Okay, I'll give it a try.

Dr. B: Olivia, you said that it was upsetting that Michael was sullen and withdrawn. **Why would it bother you** when that happened?

Olivia: To me that would mean that he wasn't interested in me or my needs.

Dr. B: So **why would it bother you** if he wasn't interested in you or your needs?

Olivia: Then I would feel all alone.

Dr. B: **Why would it bother you** to be all alone?

Olivia: Many times when I was young, after my parents were fighting, my mother would become withdrawn. Just to see if she was mad at me, I would ask her to help me with something. She wouldn't answer and sat there looking down at the floor. To me, that meant that she didn't care about me. I always worried that if I really needed help she wouldn't be there for me.

Dr. B: And **why would it bother you** if she was never there for you?

Olivia: If I was young and helpless I would die. I know this isn't logical, but I think that I often did get frightened of dying when I was a little girl.

Dr. B: Okay, Michael and Olivia, you can begin to see how you have been unknowingly frightening each other. That fear then led to the crocodile response of fighting or withdrawing. Now I'd like show you some ways to bring your owls in charge when you talk to each other. I want you both to try it, so that you'll get to see the thoughts and feelings involved here. I would like you to "replay" any of the fights that you've had before, but now using the ideas that I've mentioned. See if you can point the discussion to a win-win ending.

Olivia: When you pull away from me, you make me feel all alone. You need to help me with that.

Michael winces and begins to pull away and lean back in his chair.

Dr. B: Olivia, I think it is appropriate for you to ask Michael for help with your feelings of aloneness. He should be your best and most important friend. But did you notice how he pulled back in his chair while you were asking him to help you? Our partners see our faces and hear our voices, but we do not. You were accurately pointing out how he was not responding to your needs. Knowing you both a bit now, I think he pulled back because he felt you were saying he was bad because he was not helping you. Let's see how you might get his owl to come out and help you. His crocodile is afraid to engage with you when you are angry and blaming.

Olivia: Michael, before I start, I want to tell you how cute you look in those old fashioned bow ties you wear. My Austrian grandmother used to call my grandfather "schatzi" (treasure) to let him know how much she cared for him. I would like to let you know that you really are a "schatzi" to me when I'm not frightened.

I don't know who frightens who first, but I do know that when you pull away from me, I get scared and desperate. I know that it brings back to me all of the fears I had as a kid, of being alone with neither of my parents being there for me. So Michael, please try to help me by not backing away from me or being angry at me.

I know that in some ways I'm just like my dad. I have a short fuse and attack others a lot. I frighten you and the children. They also get furious with me and yell and scream. I really do apologize for hurting and upsetting you and the children. Please forgive me.

Dr. B: Olivia, did you notice how your Supersensitive Neural Network sets you up to react to Michael as you did? Our Supersensitive Neural Networks in our crocodiles confuse what was past and what is present. So what was in our past then determines what we see in the present. Everyone does this from time to time.

Michael: Olivia, I've been listening to what you and Dr. B. have been talking about, and I realize that I, too, usually start our fights by telling you how mean and bitchy you are when you want something. I'm beginning to get a clue as to why my comments in the past have not worked. I was doing the very same blaming that I criticized you for. You couldn't hear anything that I said when I started my comments with telling you that you were bitchy. Then you would only scream louder.

When I sit here and listen to how hard you struggle to make this all come out well, I realize how much I do care for you, especially when you call me your "schatzi." It must be hard for you when I pout and withdraw, no matter who started it. I apologize for doing that, even though I know that I do it automatically without thinking. I am sorry.

Please help me with the fear that I'm worthless. When you get frightened and say things that I hear as an attack, I get reminded of my mother telling me that I'm not good enough to be seen by her friends. I remember getting scared as a kid that no one would ever like me. Thank you for loving me enough to marry me, have our four children, and have some great times together. If you keep reminding me that my bow ties look great, I think that we'll have a great future together!

The Healing

Michael and Olivia practiced these techniques with me and on their own. There was now hope, and there was no more talk of divorce. Olivia began her complaints with "Schatzi" and a smile, and Michael would smile. What was very touching to me was how they both were surprised with how much better they were getting along, and with how much more loving they were with each other. According to the Christmas cards they continue to send me, they will be having a great future together.

Comments to the Reader

In this story we see how automatic it is to say blaming things even when asking for help. One of the ways to avoid a blaming dialog is to have an "I" communication. When you use the word "you" the other person's crocodile may become frightened and interpret this as a blaming comment. The request for help may not be heard by your partner's owl.

An example of this is, "You are upsetting me, please help," as opposed to, "I am feeling upset. Can you please help me?"

Notice how when you use the word "you" in the request for help, it has an accusatory message which mobilizes the crocodile to respond before the owl has a chance to answer the request in a thoughtful and caring way.

Chapter 9

THE BABY IN THE BUGGY

Description of the Couple

Simon and Rita, both in their mid-thirties, apologized for bringing their baby to their first appointment, explaining that their babysitter had gotten sick. Their 5-month-old daughter Mary was sleeping peacefully. As I watched them soothing the baby during the session, it was very clear to me that they were good parents.

Simon, a stocky man, looked as if he could have been a football fullback. Simon spoke first. His face did not reveal much emotion. He said that he had agreed to come to counseling because his workaholic behavior at a small company was causing his wife much distress.

Rita, an attractive young woman, seemed agitated as Simon told his story. She frequently scowled as Simon spoke. She said that Simon did not understand how distressed she really was. Her complaints were in sharp contrast to her beaming and cooing while holding the baby. I could already see that Rita was the "fighter" and Simon the "flighter."

The Problem:

Rita said, somewhat impatiently, that she thought Simon was really very nervous about his job. What was personally very difficult for her was that he put very little energy into paying attention when she was trying to communicate with him. She said he was constantly distracted with his job and not at all empathic with her. She was clear that she didn't need him to help her, but rather that she felt lonely when he didn't engage with her. Rita also complained that Simon didn't fight fairly. Instead, he just pouted and got stubborn.

Simon said that Rita was demanding and often screamed at him. During one of their fights, she blurted out that she hadn't wanted to be pregnant. "Having the baby was your idea, not mine," she said. Simon added that he had constant feelings of insecurity about what he had accomplished in his life. Now he felt as if he was hearing Rita tell him that he was an inadequate husband.

Simon said that he was coming to therapy to be less nervous, while Rita said that she was here to make their relationship "smoother." They were intellectually aware that unless many of their issues got resolved, they could wind up with a divorce, and neither of them wanted that.

Background

Simon and Rita grew up in Los Angeles in Catholic families. Simon said that his mother was tough, independent, caring, judgmental and demanding. He described his father as a loving man, but periodically he had fits of anger. He  reported that his mother continually demanded greater achievement from Simon. Although he had many leadership roles, he still had anxiety that he wasn't doing enough.

 Rita had a much more challenging background. She reported that during her childhood, her mother "was never home because of her job." Rita said that she had felt that her mother didn't love her. She recalled her father as being playful and affectionate. When she was 10 years old, Rita's parents divorced. Rita lived with her mother. She said that during that period she often had nightmares and stayed home from school with headaches.

The Session

Dr. B: As you both have an awareness of each others bothersome behaviors, let's use our session here as a kind of laboratory to see what is going on behind the scenes. I've gone over with you how our Supersensitive Neural Network is determined as we grow up. Things that were upsetting in childhood, such as parents yelling at us, can make us supersensitive to our adult partner yelling at us. I want to show you exactly how this leads to having your crocodiles take over and initiate fights. Rita, why don't you start? Pick a recent episode that got you upset with Simon.

Rita: Well last night a typical thing happened. Simon got home from work and I was unloading the groceries. I was very tired from a long day with the baby. I asked Simon to talk to me because I missed adult talk all day while talking to the baby, and he said he would very shortly. The next thing I know, he's back on the computer doing some project from work.

I lost it and started screaming that he cares more about his work than about me.

Dr. B: Before we try to solve this problem, I would like you to see what lies behind your angry responses. In order to do this, I need to talk to your crocodile. I'll ask you some questions. Try not to think about the answer, but rather just say the first thing that comes to mind. Remember that the crocodile reacts much faster than the owl, so that the first thing that comes to mind will probably be from the crocodile. So Rita, **why would it bother you** if Simon went back to his computer ?

Rita: That would mean that he feels that his work is more important than me.

Dr. B: **Why would it bother you** if he felt that his work was more important than you?

Rita: That would mean that he didn't care about me.

Dr. B: Even though it sounds like a stupid question, **why would it bother you** if he didn't care about you?

Rita: That would mean to me that I wasn't loveable.

Dr. B: **Why would it bother you** if you weren't loveable?

Rita: Then I would be all alone.

Dr. B: And **why would it bother you** to be all alone?

Rita: I don't know if I could take care of myself. That sounds stupid, but I guess some part of me thinks it.

Dr. B: And **why would it bother you** if you couldn't take care of yourself?

Rita: This sounds stupid, but my first thought was, "I won't make it."

Dr. B: Right, some part of you thinks that you'll die. Remember than in our crocodile brain, when it "interprets" the data to mean that there is a threat to survival, adrenalin is secreted, and we go into a "fight-flight" mode. The fight begins there, before we even think about it.

Rita: You know, as we were going through this exercise, I realized that this very thing occurred with my mother when I was little. She would always go to work and leave me with the babysitter. I see now that it is almost the same thing with Simon.

Dr. B: Simon, I would like to go through the same exercise with you so that you can see what your crocodile gets upset about. What about last night's episode bothered you the most?

Simon: When Rita hollered at me, while I was trying to do my job well.

Dr. B: **Why would it bother you** if she hollers at you?

Simon: I hear that she's telling me that I am not doing well enough.

Dr. B: **Why would it bother you** if she doesn't think you are doing well enough?

Simon: I grew up feeling that my performance wasn't good enough and that I have to do better. If I didn't do good enough then I wouldn't be loved. I guess that I always felt that I was loved for my "performance" and not for me.

Dr. B: So if you are not loved because of inadequate performance, **why would it bother you**?

Simon: I see where you are going, but it's true for me also. If I don't contribute enough, then it seems life isn't worth living.

Dr. B: Of course. **Why would it bother you** if you were not loved and don't contribute?

Simon: I keep feeling that someone won't like me if I don't contribute more and so I am constantly in a low state of anxiety. When I was growing up helping around the house was not considered important. Getting good grades and achieving were where I got points. As I go through this exercise, I realize that I am listening to two voices simultaneously. One's is Rita's, which asks me to stop what I am doing and sit down and talk to her. The other, which is my mother's, tells me to work harder at my job. I think that the majority of the time I listen to my mother and not Rita! Not a good way to make a marriage work. I'm also aware that Rita attacks me by yelling and denigrating me. Then I get back at her by tuning her out, or quietly being stubborn and defiant, which only makes her more enraged.

Dr. B: To briefly review, what, in my experience turns out to be the best approach to making it a win-win:
Ask yourselves, "Who's talking now?" If you are upset, angry, or frightened, it's probably your crocodile.

Then, after taking yourself through the **"Why would it bother you**?" exercise, it is very important to not make any blaming comment to your partner since that only activates their crocodile. Instead, say exactly what you are feeling. "I am frightened" is much more skillful than saying "You frightened me."

Invite your partner's owl out by doing or saying something complimentary. Then ask them to help you.

All of us occasionally make some crocodilian comments or do things that are not kind. It is always very helpful to apologize to your partner for hurting or upsetting them as soon as you can.

Even though this may seem awkward, I would like you both, in the spirit of trying something new, to take the fight you had and try to make it come out win-win. Rita, why don't you go first?

Rita: This all feels weird to me, but I'll give it a try. Simon, you are such a good provider for me and the baby. Sometimes, I interpret your attending to your job as meaning that I am not very important. This scares me. Please help me with my fears about being inadequate to raise children. Also please forgive me for all the times that I called you a lousy husband.

Simon reached out and squeezed Rita's hand affectionately.

Simon: I guess it is my turn. Rita, even though you don't think that you are a good mom, I think that you are. I always walk around feeling that I am not doing well enough on the job or contributing enough to society. I know that this is my stupid crocodile talking, but it gets very loud in my head and then I get doubly frightened that I am doing the husband job poorly. Please help me with this in any way you can. I guess the way I handle my fears leads me to hurting you. I pout or I don't pay attention to you and the baby when I am home. I do apologize for this.

The Healing

Since finishing counseling with me, I periodically hear from Simon and Rita, usually to report good news. Using the approaches we had practiced together and improvising on their own, their relationship continued to improve. They had two more daughters and Rita enjoyed mothering. Simon paid more attention to Rita, and he spent more time with his family.

Comments to the reader

More often than not, in relationships, our crocodile fears override our more loving owl nature. When this happens we are unable to be intimately involved with our partners.

In this story we see how Simon's owl knows that Rita wants him to be loving and caring about her. He also wants this, but, his irrational crocodile fears that if he takes the time off from work, he will be in danger of not being as successful as he thinks his mother would want. Then she would criticize him and not love him and "he would die." In Simon's case, his loving owl nature is overridden by his frightened crocodile.

Chapter 10

HARRIED HOUSEWIFE

Description of the Couple

Michelle, a 34-year-old attractive brunette, was dressed casually, and my sense of her was that she was nervous and worried. Peter, her husband, was a tall, handsome man wearing khaki slacks and a white sports shirt. Even though he was a few minutes late, he seemed completely relaxed. They had arrived in separate cars and Michelle chided him for not being there on time. Peter explained that he'd been late because he'd been in a business meeting that had gone longer than he'd expected.

Michelle began telling me about their one-year-old daughter. She beamed as she took out her cell phone to show me her daughter's picture. Michelle talked about how overworked she felt as director of a small parochial school. She explained how she had to direct the school, fill in as a teacher when a staff member got sick, take care of all of the parents' complaints, and then rush home to shop, prepare dinner, and take care of the baby.

The Problem

Michelle's initial complaint was that she was overwhelmed and exhausted. She said that Peter, who often worked at home, didn't help her even though he seemed to be able to find the time to go to the local coffee shop. She said that he spent money there and elsewhere, but when she bought a new dress or something for the house or baby, he complained that she was going to "bankrupt them." As she described this area of conflict, Michelle's mouth tightened, her eyebrows furrowed, but she seemed unaware of being angry at her husband.

Peter described Michelle as tired, grumpy, and non-affectionate. He said that he worked very hard and earned more money than she did, and that he felt that Michelle frequently implied that he was not doing enough.

Background

Michelle was the fourth of six children, raised in a midwestern suburb. She described her mother as a self-centered woman who had more time for her sewing projects and book clubs than for her daughter. For all practical purposes, Michelle was raised by her older brother. Her father was away most of the time, tending to his job as financial director of a large company. Her father was a perfectionist and she and her older brother took after him in this regard. Michelle said that as a child she had been very shy and somewhat stubborn. She often felt guilty about many things that, in retrospect, she could have done better.

Peter was raised by parents who divorced when he was ten years old. His father had gone through many financial reversals and was frightened of being poor and unable to care for his family. Peter and his four younger siblings lived with their mother, who struggled financially. She was able to go back to school, become a kindergarten teacher and support her family by herself. Education was very important to his mother. She worked hard and sent all of her children to college. Peter said that sometimes Michelle reminded him of his mother, who he felt only showed him affection when she wasn't exhausted. His father was basically absent, barely coping with severe depression regarding his financial losses.

The Session

Dr. B: I believe that there are certain key issues underlying most or all relationship disagreements. In order to get at these now it would be helpful to take a recent example when things were not going smoothly between you and think together about what was really going on under the surface. Michelle, why don't you begin?

Michelle: Peter is really a great guy and I love him. It isn't so much what he does that is upsetting, but rather what he doesn't do. For instance, after finishing work at my school, I go to the supermarket to buy food for dinner and rush home to relieve the babysitter. I really want to spend time with the baby. Peter sees me rushing around and since he works at home, he could offer to either do the shopping, or help prepare the dinner. He does neither! Actually, now that I think about it, he criticizes me if I buy the more expensive organic veggies.

Dr. B: How do you feel right now?

Michelle: I guess I'm angry.

Dr. B: I would like to explore with you what is behind the anger. I want to talk to your crocodile brain, so I will ask you some questions. Try to not think of an answer. Just respond with whatever comes to your mind. Michelle, **why would it bother you** that Peter doesn't offer to help you?

Michelle: Because it means that he doesn't care about me and my needs.

Dr. B: **Why would it bother you** if he didn't care about you and your needs?

Michelle: Well, obviously that means he doesn't love me.

Dr. B: I know that this may sound stupid, but try it anyway. **Why would it bother you** if Peter didn't love you?

Michelle: That would be awful. I've tried my whole life to be a good girl—to even be perfect so that everyone would be pleased with me. I probably got the message from my older sister, who insisted that I do everything myself and do it perfectly. I do spend extra money for food so that Peter will think that I am taking good care of our family.

Dr. B: We are almost at the bottom of the anger issue. Let's go a bit further. **Why would it bother you** if you were not loved?

Michelle: That would mean that I was not loveable by anybody.

Dr. B: And **why would it bother you** if nobody loved you?

Michelle: Then I would be all alone.

Dr. B: **Why would it bother you** to be all alone?

Michelle: (tearfully) I've always been somewhat terrified about being all alone. I don't think that I could make it. I'd die.

Dr. B: That's not unusual. The fear of death or being unable to survive underlies most of our most difficult emotions. Peter, you've been quiet and very attentive. Even though you know where this is going, I would like for us to try to talk to your crocodile. OK?

Peter: OK.

Dr. B: So tell me, what is there about Michelle that bothers you?

Peter: At first, I thought that her not having any time for me was the only thing that bothered me. But now, as we are going through all of this, I realize that Michelle frequently is angry at me. She scowls a lot. When she does this, I feel that I am bad in some way and I feel guilty that I've done something bad. I've always tried to take good care of the family finances, so we don't wind up poor like my father. And she thinks that's bad also. She calls me a "tightwad."

Dr. B: So **why would it bother you** to do something bad?

Peter: I don't want to be bad, because then people won't like me.

Dr. B: **Why would it bother you** to be not liked?

Peter: I feel like I am going in circles. If no one likes me then I'll be all alone. You know, when my father and mother divorced when I was ten, I felt that my father didn't like me, because he didn't try to get me to spend time with him.

Dr. B: **Why would it bother you** to be alone?

Peter: I never thought of it before, but I guess that I am like Michelle, in that I fear being alone, although I never connected it with death.

Dr. B: OK, now I'd like to suggest that you use what has come to light with the idea that the best dialogue leads to a win-win solution; it doesn't threaten the other person's crocodile. Have a positive and non-blaming conversation where you ask for help with your worry, distress, or concerns. First, ask yourself: "Who's talking now?" If it isn't your owl, you may need to wrestle with yourself until you can spot your crocodile about to speak. The very act of noticing that your crocodile is speaking is bringing in your wiser owl to participate in the dialogue. Not feeling neutral or positive may be an indication that your crocodile is in control of you. Keep in mind the idea that behind all negative feelings lays some fear. This then can give you something to ask for help with. And don't forget to apologize for any crocodilian comments that you may have made to your partner as soon as you become aware of them. This usually can help to reduce their reactivity. Using some of these ideas as a guide, try to present your thoughts and feelings to your partner and have the conversation come out win-win. Michelle, why don't you try first?

Michelle: I guess I may as well apologize to you for upsetting you with the faces I made. I really was not aware of doing that. I also want to ask you to help me out with my problem. You really are a good guy, and I realize that I have never even asked you to help me. I guess that I thought you should realize I need help without my having to ask. I think that I also struggle with the idea I got from my older sister that I should do everything myself and do it perfectly. Well I'm scared that I can't. So please do the shopping for me on some days, and then you can spend whatever you like for food. Also sometimes take the baby when I come home, so that I can rest, take a walk, or even go to the gym. And then maybe I'll be interested in some romance in the evening. Oh my goodness, I can't believe that I said all that!

Peter: (*now smiling*) For that romance part I would be happy to give up the trips to the coffee shop.

Dr. B: Peter, just for the purpose of practicing, I would like you to tell Michelle about something she's doing or saying that is distressing to you. Try to remember the "Who's talking now" step, along with saying something positive and asking for help with your fears.

Peter: Michelle, you really are a great and caring wife. This is a hard one for me to put into words. But sometimes when you walk around, sad and almost moaning, I feel guilty for doing something bad to you and then I get scared. Please help me with this. I was almost tempted to say that you were making me feel bad. Then I remember Dr. B telling us not to blame the other person because it would stir up their crocodile. I guess that when I see you walking around sort of down, I react to it. You are not actually doing anything to make me feel guilty, but I do feel awful. I don't think that I have ever brought this to your attention. Probably saying something like, "Michelle, I feel guilty when I see your unhappy face—please help me" would get the owl-owl process in motion. I'm sorry that in the past I haven't asked you what I could do to help you.

I think about money with my father's head and fear system. I probably think that when I control the spending we are safe, but when you do the spending, I don't know how far you'll go. I know that it's not fair, but I guess my crocodile does think that way. Please buy the organic food. My owl does know that we can afford it and it will make our family healthier.

Dr. B: One of the things that can be helpful is to remember that all of us probably have a Supersensitive Neural Network and it is usually poking it that brings up old memories with their painful associations. Michelle, in your case the extra demands of marriage, motherhood, and work responsibilities pushed against your childhood Supersensitive Neural Network fears of not being perfect and therefore not loved, or not having enough money or food to survive. And Peter, you told me the other day how your dad would "guilt trip" you with a hangdog face and you would feel very bad. Your Supersensitive Neural Network was all set for Michelle's sad face to provoke the same reaction. Her spending habits provoked your fear of not having enough money to survive -- like your father.

The Healing

Peter's willingness and capacity to help Michelle when she asked for help made the next few years go very well. For Michelle it was a big breakthrough to be able to ask for help and see that, in fact, he could actually respond to her request. She then began to realize that she didn't have to be perfect to be loved. Peter also learned to talk to Michelle in a non-blaming way about his feelings of guilt when she was unhappy and grumpy. This opening of their owl dialogue caused their crocodile effects to disappear more and more quickly. The "money" disagreements seemed to melt away as their owl dialogues improved.

They checked back with me from time to time when they got stuck, but just reminding them to check to see "who's talking now" helped get the healing process moving again. They relaxed enough together to have two sons and a great deal more joy between them as compassionate and effective partners.

Comments to the reader

Often we choose our partners in order to set up and thereby repeat an unresolved problem from our childhood. We unknowingly "push" our partner into a parental mold that is modeled on earlier life patterns.

In this story, Peter not only "picked" Michelle, who like his mother is hard-working and complaining, but he also unconsciously didn't help her, so that she was less affectionate and more complaining. This pushed her to be a closer duplicate of his childhood mother.

The compulsion to repeat something painful from our past is an attempt to set up and repeat the problems of our childhood but now resolve them with a better ending. Sadly, unless there is some type of intervention, it all too often has the same ending as before.

Chapter 11

SELF-CARE: THE DO-IT-YOURSELF TOOL KIT

The stories in this book have focused mainly on the healing of relationships through couples working together. However, there is a lot that you can do by yourself to increase your awareness of "Who's talking now?" and positively affect your relationships.

Lessening Your Fear and Anger

Often, when we are flooded with the negative emotions of fear and anger, in the confusion of the moment our crocodiles say or do things which are destructive. Try to slow things down and ask yourself, "Who's talking now?" This will help to give your owl time to come into the exchange, so that you can handle the situation more skillfully. Once your owl is in control you can use the **"Why would it bother you**?" question to help lessen your fear and anger.

Try it now. Imagine yourself in a situation in which you reacted with anything from annoyance or irritation to rage. Then ask yourself, "Who's talking now?" If you can see that it's the crocodile, ask yourself, "Why does that frighten me?" Notice that you use the feeling of anger as a signal for the owl brain to inquire about your fear. The first few times you may see that your response is something like, "I'm not frightened. I am furious." It is very important to not let yourself off the hook, but continue until you recognize the fear that is under the anger. You may want to write this out or say it out loud. Ultimately, you will understand that your response was your fear of death.

It is clear to me that often I would rather stay annoyed and be righteously angry, as that would be my unskillful crocodile's way of not getting "hurt" again. My **SNN** is prompting my crocodile to say, "**SEYMOUR!** You have been hurt before! Use your anger to keep the enemy at a distance."

Don't give up. Keep pushing the questioning to get behind your anger and discover what is really bothering you.

For example:

Owl Question:	Why are you so afraid of being involved?
Crocodile Answer:	They will reject me.
Owl Question:	**Why would it bother you** to be rejected?
Crocodile Answer:	It would be terrible to be alone and scared.
Owl Question:	**Why would it bother you** if you were alone and scared?
Crocodile Answer:	I think that I'll die.

Many times I have done this exercise on myself even though I know where it's going. I could just jump ahead and say, "I see the fear of death" and short circuit the exercise. But, it is important to actually say the sequence of questions and answers to achieve the best results.

This process has proven useful to me on many occasions. For example, one rainy night, my wife asked me to go to her car in our uncovered driveway and take her suitcase out of the trunk of the car. She had left the zipper open and when I grabbed the suitcase in the dark most of the contents fell out on the wet driveway.

I was furious. My crocodile was shouting, "How could she have been so thoughtless? She is so careless! Why would she have sent me out on such a stormy night?" Then my owl answered "Listen Seymour, it's not even your stuff that got wet. What's the fear behind the rage?" My very next thought was, "My mother will yell at me because the clothes are wet and dirty." It was my **SNN** at work, confusing my past with the present. In listening to this inner dialogue, my rage went away quickly. I smiled. The moment I was able to get to what the fear was about, I went from rage to caring and warmth for Sylvia. When I went back in the house I told my wife, "Sweetie, please help me by being careful about the zipper in the future." She smiled back and said "I am so sorry that I caused you all that extra work."

<u>Self Care</u>

Caring and nurturing of yourself will strengthen the wisdom and caring of your owl so it can have a greater chance to show itself. The following is not a complete list of ways to do that, but rather is a starting place.

Exercise

As we know, exercise is important for physical health, but it is also very important for mental health. When the exercise is vigorous enough, your brain signals the body to produce endorphins, a hormone in the brain that is a great antidepressant. Feeling strong and vigorous will help you feel less vulnerable and have less need for your crocodile to be on guard for danger. Exercising on a consistent schedule is not only important for you, but for your relationships also.

Sleep and Rest

Do you notice that when you are tired and not getting enough good sleep, you tend to be more grumpy and have a shorter fuse? Our crocodiles stay on guard no matter how much sleep you get, but our owls, with inadequate rest, lose power to stay engaged. In general, seven to nine hours of sleep would be ideal, or shorter times with daytime naps.

A Healthy Diet

A balanced diet is crucial as it supplies adequate and useable supplies of energy to our brains. Just as they do with lack of sleep, our crocodiles stay on guard with lack of food. However, reasonable owl thinking can be impaired by such things as low blood sugar, a problem that is compounded by a high sugar diet. Grumpiness, a crocodile trait, can greatly increase, along with depression, when our blood sugar level is out of balance.

Bodywork Disciplines

Wilhelm Reich, a noted early psychoanalytic pioneer, recognized how memories could be held in what he called body armor. In general, the traumas coming from very early in life can be difficult to find and fix. You could think of this body armor as solidified crocodile muscle that has developed to prepare for danger. In his excellent book, *Yoga and the Quest for the True Self*, Stephan Cope describes the many ways that a yoga practice involving muscle tension and breath can gradually reach and get through the deepest layers of armor to release us from the early traumas in our thoughts and feelings. Then, as adults with the owl maturity, we can better understand what's happening to us. Other valuable body therapies worth mentioning include Rolfing, Feldenkrais work, Tai-Chi, and martial arts training.

Prayer, Meditation or Other Spiritual Practices

It's important to keep your mind in a positive mood. Belonging to a church group, a meditation group, a fellowship group of any kind that supports the owl's awareness of what it is thinking is an important prerequisite for doing the right thing. Strengthening this awareness reduces the power of the crocodile to take over.

Books, seminars, and meditation retreats all provide a means to strengthen your owl functions.

There is one practice that I personally use and find very helpful. It is called Metta, a Pali word that means loving kindness, and comes from the Buddhist tradition. The most simplified version is, "May I Be Happy; May I Be Peaceful" or "May You Be Happy; May You Be Peaceful." When I am in an emotionally challenging situation or know that I am about to enter into one, I start the repetitive mantra in my mind silently. I find that it keeps my owl out and engaged while calming my crocodile.

There is another practice, coming from the orthodox Jewish tradition, called *Mussar Work*. A good introduction to this is in *Everyday Holiness* by Alan Morinis. Mussar actively helps to illuminate crocodile activity, and lessens or eliminates it with the help of inspirational readings and daily exercises focusing on our interactions of everyday life. This work is done with a teacher, study partner or even by oneself. As you see the impediments (crocodile behavior) to your caring self appear, you will want to eliminate or lessen them to attain the joy that lies underneath.

The Work of Byron Katie is another method of self inquiry that can very powerfully illuminate the forces in our mind that keep us from happiness and love. Her book, <u>Loving What Is</u>, presents a series of four questions that one uses to focus on the false beliefs that perpetuate negative and unhappy mind states. Once these mind states are revealed, Byron Katie then shows how they can be reversed.

Here are two stories that I learned from spiritual teachers that I call to mind often to keep me in a hopeful mood.

First:

The Chinese Farmer: A Chinese farmer had a horse and felt that he was fortunate because he could plow some fields. One day his horse ran away and the farmer said, "Now I am unfortunate (crocodilian pessimism) because I cannot plow my fields." The next day the horse which had run away returned, bringing with it a wild horse. Now, the farmer said, "I am very fortunate because I have two horses and can now plow more fields."

He asked his son to tame the wild horse so that it could also plow the fields. When the son got on the wild horse, the horse bucked, threw the son to the ground, breaking the son's leg. Now, the farmer said, "I am unfortunate again (crocodilian view) in that my son broke his leg." The next day the king's army came by the farm looking for recruits to go to war. But the farmer's son could not go to war because he broke his leg. Now the farmer said "I am fortunate because my son has been saved."

And so the story of life goes. We really don't know what will be fortunate or unfortunate.

Second:

Three Ditch Diggers: Three men were digging a ditch and doing the exact same thing. The first digger, when asked, "What are you doing?" replied glumly and grimly, "I'm digging a ditch." The second ditch digger, doing the same thing, seemed much happier. When asked, "What are you doing?" he replied with some joy, "I'm helping to build a building." The third ditch digger, also doing the same thing, was practically dancing on the shovel. When asked "What are you doing?" he replied with an inspirational sigh, "I'm participating in the creation of an empire." By changing how we perceive what we do, we can move from feeling grim to feeling inspired and joyous.

Medication

Psychiatry has moved from the era of Freudian psychoanalysis to that of neuroscience. Along with this has come the development of medications that can help tame the extremes of anxiety, anger, and depression.

I believe that the most significant development has been the class of drugs called SSRIs. A well known example is Prozac. In addition to being prescribed for depression, they have been found to be very valuable in reducing fear and aggression. For some people they can reduce crocodile hyper-aggression which may come from the hurts of early life, and/or genetic factors that we may have inherited from our parent(s). Some people need to be tested for certain hormonal or endocrinal disorders which could be contributing to hyper- aggression. These could be helped or cured with properly indicated medications, which would require a medical investigation by a specialist, such as an endocrinologist.

Conclusion

HEALING RELATIONSHIPS/HEALING THE WORLD

In this book and in my practice with couples, I make the assumption that when we live from a place of caring and friendliness, we will have the greatest happiness and joy in life. We must learn to enable our owl minds to take charge of our communications with those we love. A life ruled by crocodile anger, mistrust and non-caring, seems to be a recipe for an unhappy, unfulfilled life.

In this book, you have been exposed to a new way of navigating the challenges of relationships. Asking yourself the question "Who's talking now?" can help you recognize the central issues that are causing your concern. Any negative feelings would show that the crocodile is out and in charge.

I would like to review and summarize the five new thinking tools that have been presented so far. These need to be mastered, in order to improve your relationships.

Question Yourself

What am I *feeling?* If it's anger or its derivatives, ask yourself, "What is the fear that is under the anger that caused the crocodile to come out?" The fear can be tracked to its roots of fear of dying with the **"Why would it bother you**?" line of self questioning.

Make Friends

It is crucial to *first establish a friendly atmosphere* with a touch, a smile, or humor, or any other things you discover within your own style.

Say Your Fear

Tell your partner "I am worried or concerned or frightened" about… (e.g., not being loved, or dying). In using this tool it is important to *not to blame your partner,* which can bring out their crocodile. Towards that end, try not to use the word "you."

Ask For Help

Ask your partner, *"Please* help me." By giving your partner the power to help you, it is more likely that their owl will come out. It's a way of showing that you trust them and that you are not a danger to them.

Repair The Rupture

Here we try to repair the inevitable crocodile errors we all make. It's important to take responsibility for knowingly and unknowingly upsetting and/or hurting your partner. Somewhere in the apology, it is important to say "I am sorry for causing you distress, upset etc." It is important to own it!

Our Journey Ends --- and Begins

I hope the stories and methods I suggest in this book have helped you see your relationship as a wonderful opportunity to bring to the surface your crocodile brain issues to be looked at, worked on, and resolved so your owl brain can lead you to a fulfilling life.

You might ask, "Is there a place for aggression and spontaneity in a relationship?" Absolutely! But, it is important that you have a trusting relationship with each other within which the tickle, joke, poke, pinch, tease and even put-down are seen as part of playfulness with a loved one (owl). A relationship in which the partners trust each other to stay in the relationship allows each of them to experience a complete array of human emotions. The wife of the Archbishop of Canterbury, in response to a young person's interview question about whether or not in her long marriage she had ever considered divorce, responded, "Divorce, never! Murder, frequently." Here we see the owl and the crocodile speaking in the same sentence. In passion and in sex, there is often a place for some aggression, hopefully under the direction of the owl, but certainly not if it is seen by your partner to be threatening.

The approaches described in the previous chapters will be helpful to people who are functioning reasonably well most of the time. There are situations and circumstances where more than what is offered in this book is needed and professional help should be sought.

Those who abuse or are abused by physical violence or severe ongoing verbal violence should immediately seek professional help. Severe ongoing verbal abuse that is not controllable should also be a signal for a similar effort. This book will not be of help in situations where drug and alcohol addiction are present. Professional help is essential, which may require hospitalization, rehabilitation centers, medications, and such programs as Alcoholics Anonymous or Narcotics Anonymous. When they are reasonably successful, *then* this book can be of help. When ongoing promiscuity is a problem, these individuals usually have a sense of entitlement, which they feel gives them a right to violate the usual social contracts that most couples have. This severe self-centeredness, or narcissism, is a sign of a crocodile out of control. If they want to change, then with skilled psychotherapy there is hope. Unfortunately most of these individuals do not want to change and their destructive relational and worldly problems continue.

Though the tools I have identified in this book are simple, I know they are not easy to use. However, the rewards can be great when effort is made. Not only are we struggling with problems that came from our lifetime, but also with hundreds of thousands of years of evolution of our crocodile survival brain. We need to be patient with ourselves and with our partners.

In closing, I would like to tell you a story about Pablo Casals that will help when your progress seems slow. Casals, thought to be the world's greatest cellist in some circles, still practiced four to five hours each day when he was eighty-six years old. When his friends would ask him why he still practiced so much, he said, "I think I'm making progress." I believe you can continue to grow and make progress until the time of your death.

I finished writing this book during a very heated political campaign and I realized that the "Who's talking now?" approach was helpful to me as I listened to the speeches of candidates and pundits and felt my responses to what I was hearing. When I felt strong responses in myself, particularly antagonistic responses, I was able to see how my crocodile had been frightened. I thought about how fear operates on a worldwide scale - as it does in relationships – in ways that cause otherwise well meaning people to make unwise choices. I thought about how different it would be if the world was full of people whose owls were in charge!

There are those who are blessed with parents who taught them, by example, the importance of empathy and caring about the feelings and needs of others. It is important that children not taught these things be given early training with wise, loving and caring preschool teachers. I was very encouraged recently to hear about The Serra Preschool in San Francisco, which has been teaching exactly this for the past 35 years (www. TheSerraPreschool.com)! Also George Lucas's EDUTOPIA (www.Edutopia.org) is involved in social/emotional learning in the Kindergarten to 12th grades. These additions to regular academic learning fill a crucial need of our society.

I am also encouraged by the writings of economist Dr. David C. Korten who, in his book *Agenda For A New Economy* (2009), spells out how to change the world economic system from one based on crocodile fear values to one based on owl caring values.

I want my children and grandchildren, as well your children and grandchildren to live in a better world than the one I see around me now. In my view, wars, poverty, hunger, fear, sickness and lack of adequate medical care, global financial depression, chaos, and the climate change which threaten our planet are all derived from crocodile actions. The limbic system that evolved to help us survive may be slowly killing us with the internal stress and external damage it produces. The fear that leads to greed for material things and the desire for power activates our cortisol hormone system, which over time will damage our important vital organs.

Now is the time for as many of us as possible to do what we can to help humanity reach the tipping point that will lessen our crocodile behavior and greatly increase our caring owl behavior.

May each of you find within yourself your highest caring and loving values, and bravely pursue them.

It is up to you!

Works Cited

Cozolino, Louis. *The Healthy Aging Brain: Sustaining Attachment, Attaining Wisdom.* New York: W. W. Norton & Company, 2008. Print.

Damasio, Antonio R. *The Feeling of What Happens: Body and Emotion in the Making of Consciousness.* New York: Harcourt Brace & Company, 1999. Print. Note(1) Page 54

Goleman, Daniel. *Emotional Intelligence: Why It Can Matter More Than IQ.* 10th Anniversary Paperback ed. 1995. New York: Bantam Books, 2005. Print.

Goleman, Daniel. *Social Intelligence: The New Science of Human Relationships.* New York: Bantam, 2006. Print.

Hendrix, Harville. *Getting the Love You Want: A Guide For Couples.* 20th Anniversary ed. 1988. New York: Henry Holt and Company, 2008. Print.

Hendrix, Harville, and Helen LaKelly Hunt. *Getting the Love You Want Workbook: The New Couples' Study Guide.* New York: Atria Books, 2003. Print.

Katie, Byron. *Loving What Is.* New York: Three Rivers Press, 2003. Print.

Korten, David C. *Agenda for a New Economy: From Phantom Wealth to Real Wealth.* San Francisco: Berrett-Koehler Publishers, Inc., 2009. Print.

Morinis, Alan. *Everyday Holiness: The Jewish Spiritual Path of Mussar.* Boston: Trumpeter, 2007. Print.

Salzberg, Sharon. *Lovingkindness: The Revolutionary Art of Happiness.* Boston: Shambhala Publications, 1995. Print.

Stephen, Cope. *Yoga and the Quest for the True Self.* New York: Bantam Books, 2000. Print.

Seymour Boorstein has been a practicing psychiatrist since 1959 and an Associate Professor of Psychiatry at the University of California, San Francisco, School of Medicine since 1972.

He credits working with couples for many decades, as well as his long-term marriage and subsequent parenting and grandparenting, as having shaped the unique and highly effective methodology he presents in this book.

CPSIA information can be obtained
at www.ICGtesting.com
Printed in the USA
LVHW071012020620
657221LV00011B/654